Petals of Life

Poems

Reproduced from the original edition.
This edition © BGA Publications, Amsterdam, the Netherlands, 2023.
All rights reserved.

Cover design: Meryl Tihanyi.

George Adamski lectures at the Little White Church, Laguna Beach, 1933.

George Adamski and the Royal Order of Tibet

Around 1926 George Adamski (1891-1965) had a successful business as a house painter based in St Paul, Minnesota, when he was presented with an opportunity to teach. Adamski once intimated that he studied in Tibet as a boy[1], and perhaps that was why he had always sensed teaching as his destiny. But, until the opportunity arose, he says, "I did not have the faith or nerve, to express before the public."[2] Yet, Myrah Lawrance, a well-known local psychic, told him he should leave St Paul, saying: "You'll be world famous."[3] However, Adamski says, "I had financial security in my business and there was no assurance of that in the new field. Through no fault of my own, something happened to the business and it fell apart, so I was forced into the new field".

He began lecturing as a 'wandering teacher', visiting settlements around California, New Mexico, and Arizona during the winter months, when farmers had little to do and were happy with any form of diversion: "There was no TV then and people were grateful for lectures or entertainment of any kind."[4]

By 1928 Adamski had settled in Los Angeles, teaching metaphysics classes from a studio apartment at 213 South Broadway. Here he established the Royal Order of Tibet and in 1932 published *The Invisible Ocean*.[5] In this little treatise, his first publication, he explains,

---

1   George Adamski, 'Private group lecture for advanced thinkers'. Transcript of lecture in Detroit, May 4, 1955, p.15. See also *The Invisible Ocean* p.21, where he first mentions "the masters of Tibet".

2   Adamski, 'The Destiny and Purpose of Man' (n.d.; 1930s).

3   Richard W. Heiden, 'New light on Adamski'. *Fortean Times* #333, November 2015, p.68.

4   Lou Zinsstag and Timothy Good (1983), *George Adamski – The Untold Story*, p.6.

5   Gerard Aartsen (2019), *The Sea of Consciousness*, p.24.

in beautiful simplicity, the fundamental nature of consciousness and the universality of Life – notions that are only now receiving serious attention and corroboration through quantum theory, systems science, and astrobiology.

A follower of the Indian guru Baba Premanand Bharati, who taught in the US from 1902 until 1911, Adamski's earliest benefactor was Lalita (Maud) Johnson, the heiress of a considerable fortune from Decatur, Illinois. She was among a group of followers who joined her guru on a return visit to India in 1907[6] after establishing herself as a teacher and psychic medium in southern California, where she enjoyed "a wide prestige for her writings and lectures".[7] In her book *Transmitted Light* (published in 1937 "in association with the Royal Order of Tibet") she describes reading *The Invisible Ocean* in April 1933, after which she invited Adamski to give talks for her Order of Loving Service at the Little White Church in Laguna Beach, California.[8]

In November 1933 Mrs Johnson purchased a one-acre estate on Manzanita Drive – a 17-room property in the Mediterranean Revival style with a lecture hall and a large garden that was built in 1927 by Claude D. Bronner, a successful restaurateur.[9] While this was being refurbished to serve as the Temple of Scientific Philosophy for the Royal Order of Tibet, the Order temporarily operated from Hotel ('Castle') Green in Pasadena. The Laguna Beach 'monastery' opened its doors in January 1934 and meetings were held on Fridays and Sundays.

---

6 Gerald T. Carney PhD (2007), 'Baba Premanand Bharati and Sree Krishna – The Lord of Love'. In: Baba Premanand Bharati (ed. by Neal Delmonico PhD, 2007), *Sri Krsna - The Lord of Love*, p.lvii.

7 'Royal Order of Tibet', *The Decatur Herald*, August 15, 1934.

8 Aartsen (2019), op cit, p.43.

9 'Headquarters of Tibet Order at Beach Soon'. *Santa Ana Register*, November 13, 1933. Although the report doesn't identify Mrs Johnson as the buyer, a later report does identify her as the seller of the property; see note 16.

While the local press reports were mostly factual, in its report of April 8, 1934 the *Los Angeles Times* wrote disparagingly about a cult of "purple-clad women and golden-robed men" with "feminine neophytes in flowing purple" wandering "through Elysian gardens", while claiming that changes to the $50,000 property were projected at $1,500,000. A review of *The Invisible Ocean* in a theosophical journal from 1935 even alleges that Adamski was "peddling an oil consecrated by the Masters of Tibet" at "two dollars an ounce bottle", aimed at "collecting funds for building a two million dollar monastery" or "the adventurer's [Adamski's] pocket".[10]

The passage of time didn't do the facts about George Adamski's earliest efforts any favours either – or perhaps it was Adamski himself. A young flying saucer fan who visited Adamski in the 1950s claimed twenty

---

10 *The O.E. Library Critic*, Vol.XXIII, No.6, March-April 1935, pp.[4-5].

The property at 758 Manzanita Drive, Laguna Beach, that served as the Temple of Scientific Philosophy for the Royal Order of Tibet from 1934 to 1939.

years later that Adamski had told him the Royal Order of Tibet was merely a 'religious' front for a wine distilling operation during Prohibition – the constitutional ban on alcoholic beverages in the USA imposed in January 1920. According to this report, Adamski confided that the end of Prohibition meant this was no longer profitable, which is why he went into the "flying saucer business".[11] However, upon inquiry the US Bureau of Alcohol, Tobacco and Firearms stated that no license to manufacture alcohol had ever been granted to either the Royal Order of Tibet or George Adamski[12], while Prohibition already ended in 1933 – before Adamski and his Royal Order moved from a studio apartment in Los Angeles and a hotel suite in Pasadena to the Laguna Beach premises.

Whether such claims originated with the wishful thinking of over-enthusiastic students, the exaggeration or misrepresentation of cynical reporters, the slander of disgruntled theosophists, or malicious attempts to discredit Adamski we will never know. Perhaps they were based on remarks made in jest by Adamski himself, and were misunderstood or taken seriously, given that he was known to often use "knock-about humour" and the "macho combination of exaggeration and self-deprecation".[13]

What we do know is that there are no written or photographic records, nor eyewitness accounts that document the eccentricity reported above, which would be atypical for Adamski's levelheaded and down-to-earth demeanour in any case. Neither do evidence or reports exist of complaints, indictments, arrests or convictions that would support allegations of Adamski selling snake oil, or they would have already been eagerly presented by his many later critics. Besides,

---

11 Jerome Clark, 'Startling new evidence in the Pascagoula and Adamski Abductions', *UFO Report*, Vol.6, No.2, August 1978, p.72.

12 Heiden, 'An Adamski Chuckle'. UFO Collective, Google Groups forum post, August 30, 2016 (see https://groups.google.com/g/ufo-collective/c/TRu5u-mFgzA).

13 Tony Brunt (2010), *George Adamski – The Toughest Job in the World*, p.13.

Adamski never owned the Manzanita property, while a Historic Resources Inventory from 1981 states that it was in well-maintained condition with "no apparent major alterations".[14]

In the early 1930s Mrs Alice K. Wells had been planning a trip to India to find the Masters of the East, but dropped the idea after hearing Adamski speak in Pasadena in 1934.[15] Instead, she became an active member of the Royal Order of Tibet in 1935, by then a fraternity of some 50 members, and would remain Adamski's loyal co-worker until his death. Also in 1935 Mrs Johnson sold the property to Mrs Marguerite H. Weir, but the Royal Order continued to operate from there, organizing both private and public meetings.[16] Besides Adamski, talks were given by Marguerite Weir, Alice Wells and others. According to an announcement in the local press, on one occasion Mrs Wells spoke "on Teachings of the Seven Masters".[17]

From January 1936 the Royal Order of Tibet published a monthly newsletter, *Universal Jewels of Life*, which was handed out for free to those attending the meetings. It is likely that transcripts of the talks were reproduced in the newsletter, while recordings were broadcast on a weekly 15-minute slot for the Royal Order on local California radio stations KFOX in Long Beach and KMPC in Los Angeles, which continued until October 1938.[18]

1936 also saw the publication of *Wisdom of the Masters of the Far East*, a concise summary of the Ageless Wisdom teaching in a question-and-answer format, and from 10 to 12 September 1937 the Royal Order organized a "festival of inspiration dramatizing the universal teachings

---

14 State of California Historic Resources Inventory Ser. No. 30-2651-17-04a.

15 Brunt (2010), op cit, p.12.

16 'Laguna Home Sold to Church Group'. *Santa Ana Register*, December 14, 1935.

17 *Santa Ana Register* announcement, January 15, 1936.

18 *Los Angeles Times* local radio listings, May 16, 1936; September 20, 1938.

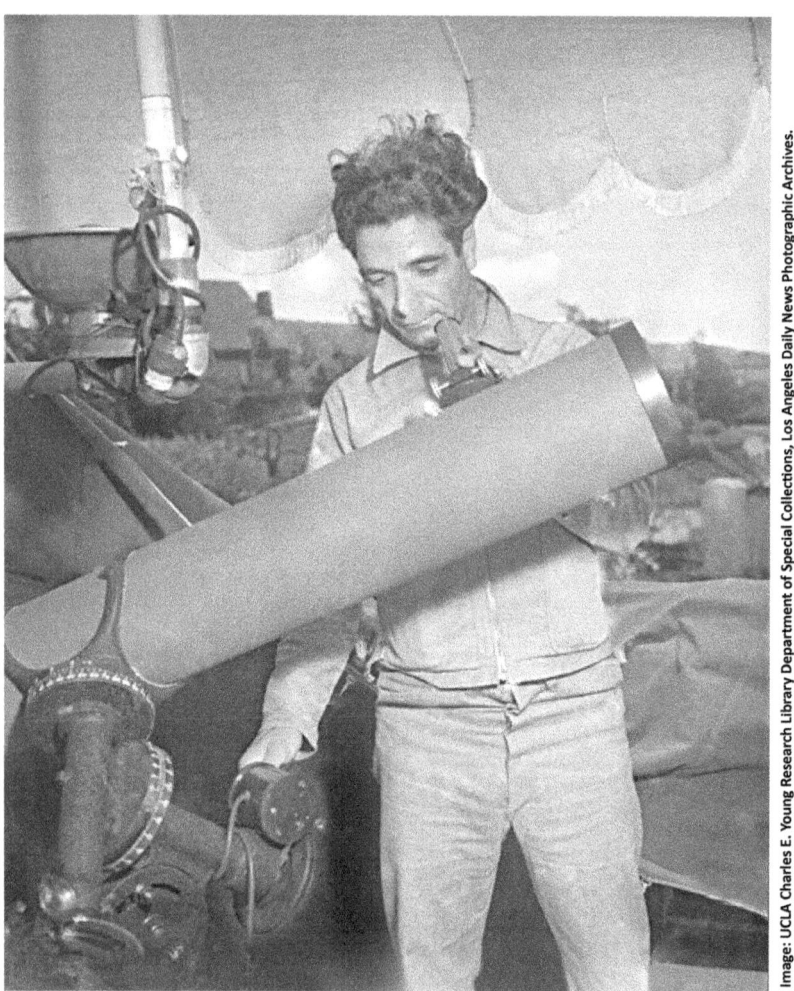

The 6-inch Newtonian telescope gifted to George Adamski, installed in a garden corner at the Temple of Scientific Philosophy, April 1938.

of the masters" that was announced in the local press.[19]

Lalita Johnson left for India for good in April 1938, to join the ashram of spiritual teacher Meher Baba, and as a farewell she gifted George Adamski a 6-inch telescope. The *Los Angeles Times* reported that it was installed "on a specially constructed platform in a garden corner" at the Temple of Scientific Philosophy, "to create an interest in the study of astronomy in conjunction with other scientific subjects. In this connection, the telescope will be open to the public on Sunday and Friday nights".[20]

For reasons we can only speculate on, by 1940 the Royal Order of Tibet was disbanded and in March that year George Adamski, his wife Mary, and some students moved to Valley Center, where they planned to build a spiritual retreat ranch named Kashmir-la[21], before moving closer to Palomar Mountain in 1944 where Adamski would focus his efforts on his interest in astronomy and extraterrestrial life, and become world famous for his contacts with visitors from space.

Most likely the twelve poems published in *Petals of Life* in 1937 first appeared in the *Universal Jewels of Life* newsletter. They exude the wisdom teaching Adamski received in Tibet, where he learned "great truths" about winning "mastery over self and soul".[22] The earliest report about the establishment of the Temple of Scientific Philosophy mentions that, after teaching there the first year, he planned to return to Tibet "for three more years of study".[23]

In Eastern philosophy and the Ageless Wisdom teaching the lotus flower and its petals are widely used to symbolize centres or vortices of

---

19 'Tibet Order to Conduct Festival'. *Santa Ana Register*, September 9, 1937.

20 'Long-Range Telescope Added to Laguna Project'. *Los Angeles Times*, April 30, 1938.

21 'Prof. Adamski to Open Dude Ranch'. *Santa Ana Register*, January 26, 1940.

22 'Tibetan Monastery, First in America, to Shelter Cult Disciples at Laguna Beach'. *Los Angeles Times*, April 8, 1934.

23 'Headquarters of Tibet Order at Beach Soon'. *Santa Ana Register*, November 13, 1933.

energy in the etheric counterpart of the human body, that progressively open as the individual advances along the path of spiritual unfoldment. The poem on page 9, 'The Lotus Flower', seems to indicate it is from this metaphor that *Petals of Life* draws its title.

It is noteworthy that George Adamski, using the honorary title of 'Professor' given to him by his students, is not named as the author of the poems, but merely as the compiler of the volume republished here (see p.xii). Perhaps this lends credence to the suggestion, from a trusted source, that these poems were inspired by the mysterious Book of Dzyan, which is seen by students of the Ageless Wisdom as an "abstract algebraical formula" of Cosmic Evolution.[24]

Whether or not that is indeed their source of inspiration, it is this very concept of cosmic evolution that lies at the heart of Adamski's lifelong teaching about life and consciousness, and these poems are no exception.

Gerard Aartsen
August 2023

---

24 H.P. Blavatsky (1888), *The Secret Doctrine*, Vol.I, p.20.

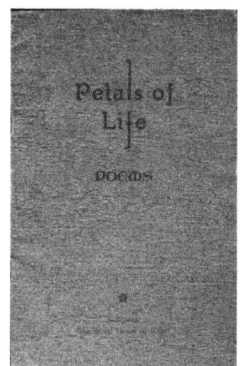

The three titles published by the Royal Order of Tibet. Adamski also published two pamphlets: 'Satan, Man of the Hour', and 'The Kingdom of Heaven on Earth'.

Petals of Life

POEMS

Published by
The Royal Order of Tibet

Copyrighted 1937
by
The Royal Order of Tibet

Compiled by
Professor G. Adamski

Invocation to the Goddess of Mercy

Goddess of Mercy, Compassionate One, thou Light
    that penetrates each living thing,
Shine not upon this mortal from afar, casting grey
    on the wall of time,
Showing the tragedy that lies within the two-fold
    consciousness of mine and thine,
But radiate throughout this house of clay and with
    thy great illuminating light
Dispell the darkness of my consciousness and purify
    my sight.

I trace far back into the ages dim the undying flames
    of transmutation;
I watch the fleeting, half-formed images passing thru
    the fires of creation.

Life after life in ascending, endless action I can see
Myself, as living images that move across the canvass
    of memory;
Life after life has this mortal sought to dwell among
    the blest
And gone back to the sightless, soundless planes
    bearing the stamp of failure on its breast.

I wander idly thru the vast arcades of space and view
    the actions of my mortal soul—
Now in the depths, now in some higher plane,
But always thou art there with thy benign and holy
    mien
In darkest moments to unveil the mystery of some
    truth I have not seen.

My mortal soul doth sin in countless ways and yet,
forever, like some tempered steel
Thou cut the strands of bondage one by one,
And with thy gentle patient hand thou guide eternally
thru all my woes and weal.

Oh merciful Goddess of undying truth, thou hold me
neither blameless nor condemn;
In thy sweet mercy thou abide unmoved, serene,
protectress of all men.

Oh grant that fear and selfishness and greed and all
the grosser thoughts that men condone
Be lost in thy illuminating grace, and purity of Truth
go on alone.

God

I see you not as Man—held in a million gripping bonds of fleshly ties. I see you as the Way—the Truth—the Light!

I utter thy true name, and then as though the very name could burn—consume the timbers of my mortal frame I lose the consciousness of earthly things. I am transported into realms of light, into the radiant glory realms of God.

I utter thy true name, and myriads of brilliant stars flash out. In rays of light they send their messages clear unto all those who are disposed to hear; proclaiming thee not Man—Not Man—but God.

The Rain Drop

I stood and watched the rain-drops come splashing
 on the ground,
And listened in a dreamy way to the sighing, mournful sound,
As forming into rivulets the hurrying rain-drops ran,
Rushing here, then coursing there, a stop! Then on
 again.

Said I, 'you litle rain-drop, you are so very small,
Pray tell me, shining jewel, why did you ever fall
In all your brilliant radiance, your purity and worth
From such a home of beauty to this cold cheerless
 earth.

'Had I been born of sun's warm rays transformed to
 realms of Light,
To float in fields of azure far above the shades of
 night,
I fain would sail forever—far from these scenes of
 strife,
In clouds of gray and silver, contented with my life.

The shining rain-drop trembled quite like a glistening
 tear
That wells from sorrow's fountain, and said, 'I come
 to bless and cheer
The drooping, dying flowers in parched and sunburned beds,
I bring them life and fragrant breath, I bathe their
 fevered heads.

'I love to work for others—for I do the will of God,
By bringing forth the life germ concealed beneath
   the sod;
By making their life brighter I am blessed a thousand
   fold,
For duty is a joy to me—such joy—cannot here be
   told.

'It is true I am pure and brilliant as any earthly gem,
But work with darker elements adds brilliancy to
   them,
And if my struggling efforts to brighten up some
   flower,
Brings happiness by serving them I cultivate my
   power.

'And all things in this Universe doth such a power
   possess,
But only by the law of love—can this gift be ex-
   pressed.
To reach above—we work below—nor lowly ones
   despise,
For only helping others up—will cause ourselves to
   rise.'

The sparkling rain-drop joined the rill that swiftly
   trickled o'er
The brown and thirsty, sun-parched earth below my
   cabin door,
Nor deemed it ought but duty, forgetting self—
   to add
A little nourishment and hope to lowly ones—so sad.

Cosmic Flame

Thy body is the shroud and hood that covers buried
    soul desires
Thy mortal mind becomes a sheathe concealing cos-
    mic fires.

In great vast domes celestial thy soul may seek in
    vain;
Immortal freedom must be earned through tests of
    joy and pain.

Great spark of life hidden so deep within these seven
    body sheathes;
Resplendent, calm, protected there, thy Cosmic Spirit
    breathes.

O holy power, great living fire which burns within
    thy house of clay—
Burn brighter, ever brighter, till all dross be burned
    away;
Till all mortality is lost in that great pregnant flame,
And on the Book of Life be written thy immortal
    name.

Riches

I have longed for a house of beauty
With furnishings rich and rare;
One beautiful room to call my own;
A place of retreat from this world of care.

I have dreamed of beautiful paintings
Wrought by a master's hands;
Rich tapestries and silken rugs
From far Oriental lands.

And of jewels and crystal vases,
Rare books from writers inspired.
Of friends and love and happiness,
All these I had long desired.

But the Master who dwelleth within
Bade me pause and take stock of my wealth;
And I saw with eyes that were opened,
And spoke thus within myself:

Do riches consist of money,
Of jewels or houses or lands?
Is happiness bought with silver or gold,
A thing to be placed in one's hands?

The coins may be few in my purse,
My house may be poor and small,
But my heart is lifted in joyous thanks
For I am rich after all.

Rich with a wealth none can take from me;
The gold of God's sunshine is mine;
The beauty of flowers and trees and hills
With their wealth of color and beauty of line.

Only the great Master-Hand could create
The wonders of earth and sea and sky,
Too marvelous even to be compared
With any painting that money could buy.

What dwelling built by the hands of man
Could compare with the Mansion of my Soul?
With that sacred inner room of peace
Where I may retire and be made whole.

The love of my friend is a jewel;
My Soul is a crystal vase
Holding the perfume of life through the ages,
Given by God through his Grace.

The Book of Nature is open to me
If I will but see and read;
The Cup of Knowledge is offered by God
If I will but drink and heed.

I may travel to far distant lands
On wings of thought free as air;
I may climb to heights never seen by man;
Those planes of Light, oh, so fair.

Poor? Ah no. I am rich
With the wealth that God doth bestow
On those who will give of their love,
And will search, all his wonders to know.

The Lotus Flower

Upon the bosom of Love's placid waters
   Thou rest in a divine and holy peace.

Untroubled by life's restless surging conflict,
   Uplifted by thy spiritual release.

Oh, Lotus Bloom, from depths of earth thou'st risen
   Thru purifying stratas of progression,
Up to the still heights where thou abide
   In glory of transcending soul expression,
The holiness and beauty of thy thoughts
   Are tribute to the Will of the Divine.

Which fashioned thee and made thee of itself,
   And poured into thee all its love sublime.

Oh, gracious and beloved thus thou art—
   A golden heart aglow with God's own light,
Soft petals unfolded in a sweet surrender,
   A flower of rarest beauty to the sight.

A lotus flower ascending to light from the depths of
         mystery,
   Enshrined thou art for all mankind to see—
The symbol of peace and sweet serenity.

Liberation

My Soul soars free as a bird
On wings that can never tire;
No bonds can ever hold me,
And I rise to planes ever higher.

I can walk in the haunts of men
With a freedom they may not see;
Walking the earth 'mid trouble and pain,
Yet my Heart and Soul are free.

Free as God, as the air—the sun—
No walls can shut me in;
My Soul goes in and out at will,
Though I walk the earth with the children of men.

The Cross could not the Master hold;
Nor the grave where His body lay;
When the sorrowing ones came the Lord to seek,
Lo, the stone was rolled away.

And an Angel in shining white
Was guarding that open door,
And the Master was free to go as He would,
To be imprisoned no more.

And when you roll that stone away
From the doorway of your mind,
The Soul will take you to Freedom beyond,
And glory and peace you will find.

All the things of the Universe
Are yours if you will but know—
Know there can never be failure or want,
And you will find that it is so.

There can never be darkness or gloom
If you open your door to the Light;
No stumbling or groping again
If you use the Soul's perfect sight.

So your Guardian Angel will keep the door
Of the mind left open and free,
If you will but trust and know
That for you no bondage can be.

The Mighty Works

Giant trees, their branches reaching heavenward;

Great buildings—man-made—towering toward the
    sky;

Winged creatures soaring into blue-gray heights;

    All earth life upward rising
    A constant transmutation
    Into finer fields of Being.

O Master power, O light divine,
Through finer purer forms thou shalt express,
Till all shall be one glorious play of light
Around the central flaming throne of Thee.

Valor

Historians write of the orators great,
    Who have won mighty victories in matters of state;
And of conquerors bold who have vanquished the foe,
    On the field of combat, thru some strategic blow,
But whoever has seen in the records of fame,
    Of the man who stood firm 'neath unwarranted blame,
Nor has fallen before all the darts that are hurled
    From the slanderous tongues of a gossiping world.

Of Napoleon's valor they've printed each word,
    But the roll-call of heroes has never yet been heard
Of the man who can laugh when his heart's being torn,
    And can keep his step light when he's weary and worn;
Or the woman who loves every beautiful thing,
    Yet in desolate want never ceases to sing;
Or the slave who can bend to a dominant will,
    And be humbled and shamed, and yet love the world still.

No, we never shall read of the many today,
    Who serving without either honor or pay;
But great valor and courage and bravery will show
    In the heart of a man—tho the world never know;
Each man is a hero and brave, in his way,
    And whether he's conquered or failed—Who can say.
Though he never is blazoned in annals of fame,
    Yet God's book of victors may witness his name.

The Song of the Within

Do you know and love your great within,
Your self of rare delight?
Do you know the language that it speaks,
Its music in the night?

Can you go within this realm of peace
Wherever you may be,
And gain the answer to your quest,
The completed plan to see?

This you may do, and more, my love,
If you will just be true
To the God self which you really are,
And let the soul come through.

For the purpose here is to recognize
That which is really you.
To harmonize with the perfect Whole,
The Father's will to do.

Your song of life will be one of love,
And joy and bliss divine,
When you learn to say within thyself
Not my will but Thine.

Progress

Out of the matrix of despair,
Burgeons the will to do and dare;

And out of the darkness of the night,
Is born the day's transcendent light;

The greatest joy is born of sorrow;
The death of today mothers our tomorrow;

The waters of life fall from darkest skies,
And oft greatest sucess from our failures rise.

Humility

Oh Father, accept this deep humility
    As reverent acknowledgment of Thee;
I ask for nought—my carnal mind is still,
    I only wait upon Thy gracious Will.

Stripped of the garment of false pride,
    I kneel before Thee nude;
Heedless of scoffers who deride
    And spurn Thy humble food.

My head is bowed before Thy mighty Love;
    All temporal things give way to things above;
The turmoil of my worldly self is stilled,
    I wait—an humble vessel—to be filled.

MONASTERY
AT
LAGUNA BEACH
CALIF.

From the same publisher

The Sea of Consciousness, feat. The Invisible Ocean
The Sea of Consciousness includes the integral text of George Adamski's lost debut *The Invisible Ocean*, two previously unpublished articles and a special clippings section documenting and demystifying his time with the Royal Order of Tibet. Plus three essays by Gerard Aartsen.
Paperback, 118 pages. ISBN: 978-90-9031695-6.

George Adamski – Letters to Emma Martinelli
Published in full for the first time, George Adamski's letters to his student Emma Martinelli, written between 1950 and 1952, shed light on this pivotal phase in his mission, and underscore the central thread of his teaching about the Oneness and universality of Life.
Paperback, 108 pages. ISBN: 978-90-830336-2-4.

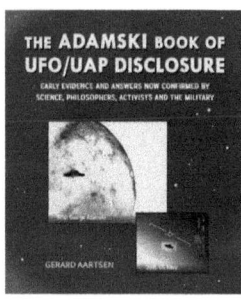

The Adamski Book of UFO/UAP Disclosure
Recent confirmations from various disciplines corroborate fundamental aspects of George Adamski's accounts and teachings, including his photographs, physical evidence, ET contact, nuclear concerns, extraterrestrial life, consciousness, and the paradigm shift. With bonus material: *We Are Not Alone in the Universe* (1958).
Large hardcover, 120 pages. ISBN: 978-90-830336-4-8.

George Adamski – The facts in context
A free website that documents the scope of Adamski's mission, the impact of his work, and the relevance of his teaching. Also features a unique illustrated biographical timeline. Visit: www-the-adamski-case.nl.

www.ingramcontent.com/pod-product-compliance
Lightning Source LLC
LaVergne TN
LVHW061605070526
838199LV00077B/7186